Khmer Girl

Peuo Tuy

peuotuy@gmail.com

For information, booking, etc. please contact (917) 744 - 6815

E-mail: peuotuy@gmail.com

On the web

www.PeuoTuy.com

www.khmergirlnyc.com

Social links

http://www.facebook.com/khmergirlpeuo

http://www.facebook.com/peuo.tuy

http://twitter.com/KhmerGirlNYC

http://instagram.com/khmergirlnyc

Editor: Timothy Prolific Jones

Book Layout: Timothy Prolific Jones

Cover Design & Interior Photographs: Manauvaskar Kublall for Media Sutra, Inc. www.mediasutra.net

ISBN-13: 978-0-9903006-0-1

Printed by Catalyst – Graphics, Printing, Binding

www.catalystgraphics.com

Table of Contents

LAOS

THAILAND

Mun River

Dangrek
Mountains

Kulen
Mountain

CAMBODIA

Tonlé Sap
Lake

Tonlé Sap River

Mekong River

VIETNAM

1

Author's Note

I have had many doubts of whether or not I wanted this book to go forward. I had many personal challenges that I allowed to interfere with the success of this book, one of which included the love of my life – my father – passing away. There are still artists and friends in my immediate circle who to this day have encouraged me to release this book. This book cannot be shelved.

When I first began my professional career as a poet, people passionately informed me that my poetry is timeless, and has the ability to touch hearts all over the world. I was told people who are going or have gone through similar struggles needed to hear my story.

The voyage of the past 30 years has been an inspiration for me to write *Khmer Girl*. I am in no way perfect, and am still working on becoming a better person, to continue to treat myself lovingly and to treat others lovingly as well. *Khmer Girl* is a victory for me, and a voice for those who have been buried beneath the traumas of self-hatred and oppression. It is a voice for all ages, genders, races, and sexual orientations.

I apologize to my family and the Khmer community if this book in any way is perceived to undermine Khmer life. I only want the world to know, especially the Khmer community, what this little Khmer girl went through.

Peuo Tuy

Preface

I plotted to eliminate, erase, rid, burn, and to kill her.

As I quietly recited this line from one of my poems, memories of my insecurities crept through my spine. All my life I battled with self-hatred, a lack of self-confidence, and low self-esteem. These battles were deeply rooted in colorism, in my hatred for my brown skin.

She is kamao. She is dark. She is black.

In Khmer (Cambodian) culture, dark automatically means ugly. Cambodians are dark and ugly. I am dark and ugly. As a little girl growing up, these oppressive words dented my soul, making being kamao the main insecurity punctuating my life throughout childhood, adolescence, and adulthood.

My skin is my enemy.

It was ingrained in my head the color of my skin was disgusting. Physically, I was never considered an attractive girl or woman according to Khmer standards. I needed to be the straight haired, skinny bodied, pale-light skinned Asian girl with wide eyes, a pointy nose, and thin lips. When summer months approached, I was to stay out of the sun or wear long sleeve shirts and a hat to cover my face so that it wouldn't darken my already brown skin. My mother made me take long baths so to scrub away all dirt and darkness in order to lighten my complexion. Covering myself with white powder and using make-up to cover up flaws and my darkness were always the norm. I was told to basically kill myself and be someone who I was not. My existence was in direct contention with Khmer customs and traditions.

Since I was always told I was extremely hideous, I felt the need to compensate in other areas. Excelling in sports, maintaining a high GPA, wearing the trendiest clothes and shoes, all stemmed from a need to create a sense of worth despite my skin complexion. I kept covering myself with lots of makeup to hide my most visible flaw. *My skin is my enemy.*

I was born in 1979 towards the end of a brutal genocide in Cambodia, which lasted four years (1975-1979). My family of eight escaped, fleeing on foot from Battambang, Cambodia, to refugee camps in Thailand. Pol Pot, the leader of the communist Khmer Rouge regime, launched a war on his own people. The Khmer Rouge evacuated the cities, and enforced a revolutionary program throughout Cambodia murdering over one million innocent Khmers. Their efforts concentrated on the highly educated — doctors, lawyers, and teachers — through starvation, disease, and execution. He manipulated children to betray their parents. Those who refused to follow his rules were slain on the spot and thrown into the Killing Fields. In 1979, the Vietnamese communist army invaded Cambodia in order to "save" the country from the Khmer Rouge's horrendous acts.

During the year of the Vietnamese invasion, my family took the opportunity to escape. We walked on foot for three days to the refugee camps across the Thai border. With hardly any food in our stomachs, we were forced to work for the Thai government, and remained enslaved for almost two years until being transferred to another refugee camp in the Philippines. Again, we were coerced to work for barely anything, awaiting announcements from the United States government, instructing us where and when we were going to be dropped. In 1983, we arrived in New Hampshire, greeted by a Presbyterian Church group who provided us with food, clothing, lodging, and a U.S. education. We were exiled from our home country and were regarded as Aliens who were Permanent Residents.

In 1985, we moved out of New Hampshire, a decision made by my parents due to the minimal presence of Khmers and Buddhists. Currently, the majority of my family is living in the second largest population of Khmers in the United States: Lowell, Massachusetts.

It has been 31 years since my family and I left Cambodia.

Our relocation to the United States was very challenging. It encouraged me at the age of twelve to journal about the simultaneous struggles of two different worlds: Khmer and Khmer American, and the inequalities of immigrant life. It was not until I reached my early twenties, having experienced discrimination, racism, poverty, and realizing the hatred I have for my dark skin color, that I needed to find an outlet to express my emotions and to find solutions in order to heal.

Growing up Khmer in America was overwhelming, and a difficult process during childhood and adolescence. On the one hand, growing up embracing Khmer culture, customs, and tradition instilled a great sense of pride. On the other hand, I was a child growing up in America, and these two worlds were at odds.

Being Khmer in America meant going to the beach on hot summer weekends scrounging for snails, crabs and mussels, steaming them immediately, dipping them in our sour salt ground pepper sauce. It also meant driving off the interstate highways onto the shoulder, climbing apple and pear trees making a salt, sugar, crushed fresh pepper dipping condiment to accompany it. It meant cooking delicious Khmer food and eating with our bare hands off the floor while sitting semi-lotus on our plastic woven straw mat. It meant incorporating some aspects of Buddhism which included my parents teaching me to never lie and steal, to treat others the way you would want to be treated, to never cheat, to always give, and to respect your elders. It also meant girls and women have less privileges than boys and men. It meant culturally, Khmer parents were stringent with their children, and with these strict rules they made sure traditions remained in the family line.

I grew up in an emotionally challenging household that did not always provide a positive outlook on life. Everything had to be perfect, love was not physically shown, and yelling, screaming, and put-downs were hurled at anyone who did not succeed. I was constantly called a loser, good-for-nothing, and eventually I would inflict the same type of emotional and verbal abuse against my family and the ones I love. Love was expressed through insults. The purpose of put downs was to motivate you to strive to do better next time.

As a young Khmer girl, I was to stay home and be obedient while my younger brother was allowed to go out with his friends. Young girls were required to abide by rules and accomplish daily chores such as cooking, cleaning, and taking care of younger siblings. Khmer boys barely had any responsibilities. We were not allowed to date. If I had a boyfriend and my parents found out, I was to be married to him so that I would not be considered promiscuous and a disgrace to the family and the Khmer community. Wearing clothes that were too revealing, such as a tank top or a mini skirt, were considered un-lady like, thus I had to dress to make sure I was covered. *Cover up real well and don't expose that dark skin.*

Attending an all-American school was another obstacle. I went to a predominately white elementary school. I was a totally different girl outside my Khmer household. I was the *American-only girl.* Because home was too harsh for me and there were many rules that I had to abide by, I felt I had to make up for it in school so others will see that I am not just any girl but a phenomenal American girl. I fought harder because my family told me I wasn't good enough. I forced myself to study really hard to get straight A's. I wanted all the white teachers and classmates to accept me. I tried to succeed in everything: art, music, athletics, math, social studies, science so that I would win friends, so that I would not be judged as some foreigner who couldn't make it, or be another statistic of "those people." I abandoned writing and reading Khmer and took up the English language full-time. I even bought my white teachers and white classmates nice gifts on all of the American holidays using my family's welfare money and the money we made from picking cans. I wanted everyone to accept and validate me. *I was the American-only-girl.*

In 1997, I began my first year in college at the University of New Hampshire. It was here that I took a few introductory English courses that provoked me to write prose about my life as a refugee and young Khmer girl growing up in America. My English professor encouraged me to keep writing, and highly recommended I get my story published in the school newspaper. I did not follow through with her recommendation, nor did I continue writing about that topic. Unhappy with the campus atmosphere, in 1998, I moved and ran away to New York City in order to find my identity (and to run away from the Khmer strict culture). I became a member of a few activist organizations, hoping they would support me in my quest to find my identity and also studied ethnic and woman's studies courses to see if any of the historical inequalities of other racial groups or my gender would assist me. After a few years, I realized that participating in activism or studying specific college courses did not have a big impact on my quest to find this self-love and self-identity. My struggle with self-hatred continued. The final stepping stone to realizing that I needed to love myself was when I became involved in a romantic relationship with a dark skinned African-American man.

Because I was insecure with my skin color, one outlet (prior to writing poetry) I turned to was developing romantic relationships with dark-skinned African-American men. Dating light-skinned men activated my insecurities, for they would remind me of how unattractive I felt and of how miserable I had been feeling all these years because I was not born with a light complexion. The African-American men I chose to date, for the most part, did not insult, denigrate the way I looked, or make fun of me. They would always let me know I was beautiful in every way, including my brown complexion. On the contrary, the Asian-American men I had romantic relationships with or even the Asian-American male friends I had during my high school years, told me they wanted to date Asian women who had sleek straight hair, slim, Chinese-looking face with porcelain skin. The beauty requirements for Asian-American woman were detrimental to the way I physically viewed myself for over two decades.

When I entered into a serious relationship with an African-American man (who I also lived with), he made me realize I was battling with issues of self-hate and finding my true identity. After having had countless arguments about race, color, and interracial relationships, he convinced me that I had not only issues with self-hate and finding my identity, I also had issues with dating men from other ethnic backgrounds due to the fear of not living up to the standards of Khmer marriage, as well as fears of failure and rejection. All of these insecurities stemmed from being self-conscious about my skin color. Because I was emotionally and mentally abused, I projected all of my problems onto the people I loved the most, and shifted responsibility to those in my circle for how I was. I hated who I was. I tried to lighten my skin color, to straighten and dye my hair; I even considered plastic surgery. I had a million and one insecurities, and desperately needed an outlet through which to heal and grow. Turning to poetry allowed me to finally love myself.

In 2003, before completing my Bachelors of Arts Degree at the City University of New York at Hunter College, I wrote "I Am Not Your Asian Exotic". The idea for this poem came from a paper I compiled for an independent studies course about how the notions of European beauty affect women of color physically, emotionally, mentally and about how many women of color are forced to compete for one type of beauty in this American market: blond hair, blue eyes, skinny body, tall, light skin. This paper helped me further realize my insecurities and the possible thousands of women who were going through similar struggles. I wanted to be an advocate for change and wanted desperately to tell the other women in this world that we do not need to change ourselves in order to love ourselves. I began to do this by portraying my story through story-telling poems.

I remember my first performance. I was terrified. I was not really ready to reveal my insecurities to the world. Swallowing my pride, I exposed all my flaws. I performed "I Am Not Your Asian Exotic", through a stream of tears. When I finished, the congested pain lifted off of my hair, my chest, my body, and most of all my skin color. *I am free.*

"I Am Not Your Asian Exotic" inspired me to continue writing more poems, eventually after a few years, it helped me create my first poetry book, *Khmer Girl. Khmer Girl* tells the story of a young girl trying to find self-love. This book is about family upbringing, romantic relationships, finding self-love, releasing self-hate, my mother, the death of my father (who passed away in spring of 2008), and more. *Khmer Girl*, along with the support from other women, books, seminars, partner relationships, meditation and yoga sessions, comrades, and friends were the primary healers that prevented me from committing suicide.

I am kamao. I am beautiful.

Bok,

I dedicate my heart,

tears, and this poetry book to you.

Herstory Begins..

...in the Land of the Killing Fields,

where bombs are embedded underneath soil
wet crystal drips from her dead shot eyes

...in the jungle fields,
she is on her father's worn-out back
hiding from stray bullets
ducking grenades and bombs
she keeps weeping

...near land mines, she screams:
Pa gum chon ga lanh ning!
Father, please be careful not to step there!
she sees a man with only one leg
bleeding profusely

...on strangled dirt roads that never end
feenin' for country mice
she is starved
bones stuck-out

...in swamps that have no mercy:
malaria-bitten
leech-eaten
she sobs quietly
her crystal drops are now lightning

...in refugee camps,
mesmerized by her mother's birthing pain
she pats her mother's disheveled head,
Ma, it's almost over. This genocide is almost over, Ma!

...on America's Emergency planes,
lifted from Thailand and the Philippines
I close my red-shot eyes
trying hard not to dream about

decapitated heads
severed legs
amputated arms

But I can't
they keep coming...
they keep coming...

...24 hours later...

I am in a New Hampshire colonial home?
fire burning
white snowing
Christian converting
speaking fluent English
trying to manipulate me to read the Bible

I remember putting on
my sun-flowered curtsy dress
little ruffled-white hat
and a big Kool-Aid smile
to convince the white people
I am just like them
ready to allow
Jesus to be my savior

But they don't know,
daddy is making plans
to move us to a place where other
Asian people live

My story shifts to the ghettoes of Lowell, Massachusetts
where rats run aimlessly through cold nights,
where hallways are always richly infested with cockroaches,
where a one family apartment converts into a 4 family household

The living room becomes:
     a bedroom
     a newborn baby's room
     a kitchen

It was here that I practiced rituals at 10:
     cooking
     cleaning
     childrearing
I was taught to be a womyn very quickly

At home, my mother used to make me concoct:
     ginger root
     lemon grass
     kaffir lime leaf
to make our famous Khmer curry
cooking was a curse – I wanted to go out and play!

After elementary school,
it was mandatory that I keep the house neat and tidy
my father made me pick up after everyone
Young Khmer girls are to be obedient and subservient!
I resented my father for injecting those words in to my soul

In junior high, I was
     changing diapers
     making baby food
     lulling my nephew to sleep
I hated it with a passion! I wanted to date boys!

On religious days,
I was forced to sit on the floor
chanting to Buddha

Save me

I stopped going to the temples when I turned 16.
My father told me,
Ga Peuo! Ngain thow thanh a roerih, hai!
Peuo! You're going to go to hell!

My story begins...

...in American schools
manipulated to believe
I gotta be America's Next Top Asian Model Minority!?!

...in white suburbs,
Fuck You – You Chinks!
Why don't you go back to your own country?!?

...in America's poverty system
where welfare lines are cages
feeding us left-overs and scraps

Are you Chinese? You must be good at karate.
My, you speak English soooooo well!

...in men's exoticising eyes,
where mail order brides are an investment to wipe out our Asian eyes

I am a Womyn
I am an Asian Womyn
I am an Asian-American Womyn

Ready to fight
racist tendencies
sexist notions
uncalled for stereotypes

I am PEUO!

Confessions from Washington

TOP SECRET:
From the late 1960's to the mid-1970's Henry Kissinger & President Nixon bombed our country wiping out a possible 2 million innocent Khmer peasants. They say they needed to stop the North Vietnamese Troops who were storing ammunitions and soldiers in Northeast Cambodia. Nixon and Kissinger attempted to cut the Ho Chi Minh Trail but it was obvious - the U.S. was going to lose the Vietnam War.

We were titled Operation Menu.
They ate our country up – Breakfast, Lunch, Supper.

TOP SECRET plan, Carpet bombing, B-52s Slaughtering village life. Now we're left with their manure, blackened, no citizens left, just dead burnt up bodies, ready to be another miserable Kodak moment.

Between 1975-1979, Pol Pot & the Khmer Rouge took over by chopping heads, legs, and arms; overworking & starving his people to death. 1979, Pol Pot and the Khmer Rouge lost possession of Cambodia; Vietnam controlled Cambodia. The death toll grew to almost 2 million more, totaling a possible 4 million.

The news says, *the U.S. bombing killed as many or more Khmers as Pol Pot's Khmer Rouge genocidal platform ever did.*

They say the U.S. supported Pol Pot's Khmer Rouge genocide.

I believe it.

TOP SECRET:
Washington played a significant role in re-birthing Pol Pot & the Khmer Rouge.

So did:
Beijing
London
Bangkok
Singapore
Berlin

The U.S. lost the War in Vietnam. Shame written all over their faces; hiding behind arrogant masks determined, still, to take control of Indochina.

The U.S. supported Pol Pot and the Khmer Rouge's exile to Thailand - 20,000 to 40,000 guerillas benefited. Fear of a shift of power in Indochina, they inducted a platform of: Anti-Soviet & Anti-Vietnamese, hoping to destabilize Hun Sen, our prime minister and the Vietnamese allies in Cambodia.

The United States' ultimate goals:
1. to destroy the Vietnamese economy
2. to overturn the government in Hanoi, Vietnam

The United States' hope:
1. to gain control & power in Indochina

TOP SECRET:
1980, U.S. secretly funded Pol Pot's Khmer Rouge exiled forces through the Thai border and gave them:
M-16's
grenade launchers
recoilless rifles
high resolution satellite photographs
and more...

1980-1986
A total of $85 million supported the plan
Under pressure from Washington, the World Food Program:
$12 million

1989
Aid grew from $20 million to $24 million

1990
Bush administration requested $7 million

China estimated to spend:
$60 million to $100 million in aid
to all factions of the Anti-Vietnamese resistance

They did this for 15 years.

I grew up not knowing any of this.

I believe all of it.

Rouge Rage 1975 -1979

In camps,
refugee
re-education
concentration
they starved us to death
they overworked us for 12 hours a day

We ate worms dogs cats crickets wild mushrooms raw rice rats / mice
muddy live shrimp leaves toads tadpoles centipedes scorpions

Some of us lived
over 1 million corpses unburied spiritually

In camps,
refugee
re-education
concentration
they starved us to death
they overworked us for 12 hours a day

They made us have edema
let us die from malaria
gave us brittle bones
our shiny long hair
cut short, thinning
bodies like chopsticks
walking skeletons

In camps,
refugee
re-education
concentration
they starved us to death
they overworked us for 12 hours a day

They separated families
killed fathers
raped mothers & daughters
shot children
manipulated kids
buried us alive
made orphans

Some of us lived
over 1 million died unblessed

In camps,
refugee
re-education
concentration
they starved us to death
they overworked us for 12 hours a day

They slaughtered the educated
doctors
lawyers
professors
those who spoke English or French
patrolled our every breath
massacred light skin tone
burnt
clocks
watches
temples
hospitals
schools
shops
killed monks
destroyed Buddhism

Some of us lived
over 1 million people died without a wake

In camps,
refugee
re-education
concentration
they starved us to death
they overworked us for 12 hours a day

The Khmer Rouge
separated my family for 10 years
my mother & her son
my father & his children
my two brothers & sister
my aunts & uncles & cousins
my nieces & nephews

In camps,
refugee
re-education
concentration
they starved us to death
they overworked us for 12 hours a day

They separated my family
I will never forget.
Those nightmares come in my dreams.

Imagine

Dedicated to my Family & the People in Iraq

Imagine
Red-blooded stains sit in my mother's womb
I remember the silent sobs, the whispers
I wonder why my mother never talks about
the harshness of the camps
I cry strangled, purple blooded tears
to the sound of my mother's uncomfortable labor
I feel her pain
Ma, I feel your pain

Imagine
Naked, torn-out palms,
my father slaving day and night
for a pot of rice
I remember the silent sobs, the whispers
again and again
I wonder why my father never talks about
the insanity of the Khmer Rouge and U.S. imperialism
I feel his pain
Pa, I feel your pain

Imagine
Running disheveled and distraught
through jungles of killing fields and mine fields,
my brothers' and sisters' hearts are left in a country
that was once ours
I remember feeling the silent sobs, the silent whispers
over and over again in my head – over and over again
I wonder why my brothers and sisters never talk
about hate dripped tears
I slice my veins in utter frustration,
my family is drowning
in choked doomed hell blood of our ancestors
I feel their pain

Bong Barouh, Paoun Srei (Brothers and Sisters), I feel your pain

Imagine
my mother covering my one year old mouth,
Shhhh...Peuo, kumh yumh. Borh yumh, a Khmer Rouge salap yeurng hai!
Shhhh...Peuo, don't cry. If you cry the Khmer Rouge will kill us!

24 years later,
I do not remember
ducking
maneuvering
hiding
running through jungles and killing fields

I imagine the genocide killing my family's
hearts
souls
and spirits

Close your eyes

Imagine
Iraqi children dying, starving, homeless and crying

Imagine
Iraqi mothers' breasts, wombs, lips, kisses, love
shattered by bombs, ammunition and soldiers

Imagine
Iraqi fathers screaming at the top of their lungs
trying to save their families' lives

Imagine
Iraqis drowning in an ocean
full of somber blood
flowing in un-rhythmic patterns

Imagine
If Iraq looked like Ground Zero times 100

Imagine
If the US looked like Iraq

I no longer need to imagine

I lived it

I Came From

a land where
I am African
wide flat nose
brown skin
thick dark red lips
black curly hair

I am a mixture
of
Tibet
China
yellow- skinned

I am a fusion of
Malaysia and Indonesia
brown-skinned
civilization was called Funan & Kambuja
Indianized through
language   Sanskrit & Pali
religion   Hinduism & Buddhism

a land where
our 1st king - Indonesian
built Angkor Wat
on the backs of Khmer slaves

a land where
wearing jewelry and crowns
silk worm sarong
golden beads
on elegant dancers
are pleasing to the eye
we wear our pride
making
gold

necklaces
bracelets
anklets
earrings

a land where
ghosts haunt
spirits roam
witches fly
ancestors protect

a land where
medication
is cupping stomachs
pinching foreheads
spreading monkey balm on wounds

a land where
Cambodia used to encompass
Thailand
Vietnam
Laos
Malaysia

a land where
cultures integrate
ethnic marriages mix
khmer-vietnamese
khmer-chinese
khmer-malay
khmer-thai

a land where
foods intermingle:
coriander
curry
ginger

galangal
kaffir lime leaves
and make delicious dishes

I came from Cambodia
where I am proud to be me

Growing Up Khmer

Food Stamps & Welfare for Aliens

I grew up in Lowell, Massachusetts in the mid-80's. I remember how poor we were. I never really understood this concept but I was able to witness our hardships through our not-so-*bling-bling* life style:

My folks drove a beat up Buick
we couldn't afford a new one

my folks never brought my younger brother & I
McDonalds or Burger King
it was luxury food
we never got to dine out
it cost too much

we never received an allowance
when we asked for $1 it was always,
you always spend spend spend
money doesn't grow on trees

I wore hand-me-down Espirit or Gap clothes
3 sizes too big
I remember that white rich chick
I envied her

My parents were hardly home so my younger brother & I took care of ourselves. I was 7 and he was 5. They each worked 3 jobs for cash; unrecorded by the government:

1. Dixie Company factory for about $3.75/hr
2. on a nearby farmland during the summer & fall season
3. picking 5 cent redemption cans

8 of us were on welfare & food stamps. This aid was given to us due to our refugee status. According to our green cards, we were *Aliens with Permanent Residency*. I always thought it was weird to be called aliens. We were martians. We were not humans.

I remembered being on welfare. I thought it was the most disgraceful part of my life. Looking back it saved us from starvation, being on the streets, and having extremely dirty or ripped clothes.

I appreciated it.

In elementary school days, a few weeks before the school season would start, each qualifying child in our household would receive an additional stipend, between $50-$150, for clothes and supplies.

I remember complaining to my mother about how she needed to allow me to make my own decisions on how to spend my money. She would always refuse, "*you are too young!*"

I was 7.

When I turned 10, she granted me my wish. I spent the money very quickly. There was not one cent left in my pocket.

At 13, I was able to work for a small stipend. Again, I spent the money very quickly. I never learned how to make money work for me. I was always broke.

The other part of our government assistance was Food Stamps. To me, it was money, but in different colors. Each household was given a decent amount of food stamps to purchase only food.

We were fortunate to grow up in Lowell so we had our connections.

The Khmer community was rapidly growing. We had our own little Khmer Town, where we bought food, makeup, clothes, toiletries, barrettes, and other non-food items all with our food stamps.

My mother rarely let me touch our food stamp money. She knew how my spending habits were.

When I turned 19, I was no longer eligible to receive these benefits. A part of me was glad because being dependent on someone or something doesn't promote self-gratification.

The other part of me felt guilty.

my mother will receive less money
my mother can't really work
she doesn't really speak English

Her skills as a mother & a wife only applied in our household. Who would want to hire an old lady
who barely knows how to read, write, or speak English?

This is the United States.

When I attended college, I educated myself more on welfare & food stamps in the South East Asian community.

In 1997, with the help of President Clinton,
Cambodians all over the U.S.
were kicked off of public welfare & placed
into Work Experience Programs
this hurt many families

the older generations
never really learned how to assimilate
they never picked up a trade or a skill
they barely learned English
so many were left picking up garbage in parks
& was rewarded with a measly check from the government

I now realized why my family squeezed every penny out of the government. They knew that somewhere down the road the laws would change, therefore, some Cambodians felt it was their right to exhaust the government's aid.

the United States of America owes us
for all the millions left dead in South East Asia

My family exhausted this aid for about 15 years.
We were proud.
Really proud.

Gardening in the Ghetto

In Battambang, we were peasant farmers.

In Lowell, as refugees in America, we were still peasant farmers.

This time in the ghetto.

Our apartment was part of a row housing complex for 8 families.
One day, my father gathered the family - all 8 of us.
We need to grow crops.
We will work the back and the front yard.

The back & the front yard did not belong to us. My father did not care;
he loved farming crops & missed growing & eating our own vegetables.

Listening to him, we put on our dirtiest ragged clothes, wrapped Khmer
scarfs around our heads underneath our hats to cover our faces from the
boiling hot sun. We wore rubber flip-flops & carried our shovels.

We pulled out:
weeds
non-edible plants
discarded debris
cigarette butts
cans
newspapers
old plastic bags
& began to soften the dirt

Ma brought over seeds of:
chili pepper
eggplant
basil
tomato
cucumber
watermelon

We shoveled, softening the dirt, parting the top layer to the side and laid each seed in Mother earth's womb, segregating each crop with its family.

We
parted dirt
laid the seeds
put dirt over
parted dirt
laid the seeds
put dirt over
again
&
again
repeatedly

My job was to water our crops at night. Father said, *they eat the water better and will grow healthier.* Lugging pail after pail of water weighing what seemed a ton, my 10 year old body struggled to the back & front yard. I eventually watered them, sprinkled them, huffing & puffing out of breath.

I remember all the neighbors staring at our immigrant way; thinking it strange, *why are they taking apart a back and front yard that do not belong to them?*

We ignored them.

Everyday
we took care of our plants
nurturing them
showering them with love

We kept watching them grow.

Everyday
neighbors would
stare at us

making weird American faces
as if they had never seen a garden in the ghetto

We kept doing what we were doing.

Everyday we would keep
watering our vegetables
feeding them with our loving peasant farmer ways
neighbors would keep thinking it strange

We didn't care.

When they were ready to be picked
we picked them with enchanted faces
we didn't have to take a trip to the supermarket
our fresh vegetables were ready for us
to be cooked at home
the Khmer way.

on the dining room floor

spreading our
embroidered peacock straw mat
on our dining room floor
like a quilted blanket
on my mattress

still
we sit in semi-lotus pose
with our bare hands
nutmeg colored fingers
licking with our pink tongues
sucking the juices out
of sweet jasmine rice
dipping muddy mud fish
entangling in spicy green chili peppers
with raw chopped cabbage
& forest green cucumbers
& long beans cracked in half
engulfing every taste & bite

still
we eat with our bare hands
on the dining room floor
family style
as we have
for hundreds of years

Our $3 Chicken

Every weekend morning, my brother goes to a nearby farm and buys 4 live chickens – $3 a piece makes it $12 total with no artificial or medicated steroid injections our $3 chicken is soooo healthy.

He puts our 4 chickens in a big clear plastic bag, ties the knots tightly so they won't run away and puts them in the back of his old IROC-Z.

At home, he boils cold water in the hour glass pot. At 10 years old, I am excited! I wake up to chicken noises in our living room, *puck, puck, puck.*

Running around wildly, feathers falling on the couch, kha kha on the floor, *yuuuck! eewww!* But I didn't care! I am thrilled to have company!

Wearing crusty eyes, loose messy curls, jungle flower sarong, white cotton t-shirt, and teeth not yet brushed I run around after them squatting, catching, playing with them, practically kissing them before my brother wrings their necks and slices them with our butcher knife.

I smile, laugh, and scream, *Yah! Yah!* They are pucking and running away from me. I soon catch their wings, stopping them in their tracks.

I ask my brother if we could keep one. He demanded, *no! we need to kill them and eat them for dinner!*

After 20 minutes of running around with my friends, I gave them up to the butcher knife. Not willing to look, I half-shut my eyes, peeking a glimpse through a hole between my fingers and seeing the blood gush out from its throat. Tears start to roll down my brown cheeks

My brother, then, makes me dip one of them in the boiling hour glass pot;

holding its feet/tied upside down
dip
up and down
dip
up and down
dip
The feathers came off easily, one by one.
Poor chicken! I'm sorry but we have to eat you tonight.

I did the same with the other 3 chickens
dip
up and down
dip
up and down
dip
The feathers came off, one by one.
Oh poor chicken. I'm really sorry.

Afterwards, he slices the chickens in half and tells me to clean out the insides of the chicken. Nasty. I was not very happy cleaning kha kha but, obeyingly, I did.

We keep everything - feet, heads, butts, and private parts.

One hour later, he marinates their feet, heads, butts, private parts, and wings and puts them in the oven. He, then, chops the body into cubes and makes healthy Khmer chicken soup. With no artificial or medicated steroids injections
adding
kaffir lime leaf
garlic
rice
lemongrass
salt
sugar
msg
our $3 chicken is *soooo good*

better than the ones from the supermarket.

I happily gnawed on marinated chicken feet
mmmm....my favorite.

I wait again in silence for next weekend. My brother will get us more
$3 chickens.

I can't wait to
wake up
wearing crusty eyes
loose messy curls
my jungle flowered sarong
teeth not yet brushed
white cotton t-shirt.

I can't wait to have some more friends soon.

Cupping Cockroaches

At that time in the ghetto – 1985
our friends didn't multiply too much
but
as we kept our dirty dishes in the sink
as we left chicken blood on the chopping table
as we stained fish sauce on the white stove top
our friends began multiplying in numbers
camping in our
kitchen
living room
bathroom
bedroom
day & night

First, I was cool with it
until one day they got on my damn nerves!

One morning,
I witnessed itchy bites on my legs
I stomped downstairs opened the fridge
I knew it – sticky little black dots everywhere
OH MY GOD!
they were *SHITTING*
in my fridge!
in my father's mud fish sauce!
my sister's sweet & sour fish soup!
my aunt's rice / vermicelli curry soup!

Disgusting!
Absolutely Disgusting!
Ewwww Gross!
I was so heated!
I dumped all the dishes in the garbage!

I yelled,
"Bok, we need to do something about our little friends who are now my Enemies from Hell!"

My father,
a practicing Thevada Buddhist, swore, "we are NOT allowed to kill a soul!"

I argued but it was no use. Sadly I responded, "alright."

Im'a do an experiment.
I woke up one morning feeling oh-so-amped and ready to destroy my enemy!

During that time, my brother worked at the Dixie Company factory. He brought home dozens of Dixie cups with matching lids. I took a pair & began my scientific experiment. I screened out many of them, looking to interview only one. I finally fished the right candidate – a Big, Fat, pregnant one. Pleased with a huge grin on my face I sealed her in being extra careful not to let my father know.

I kept her shut living without hardly any food & sunlight. After a few days, guilt became a problem in my conscience and I felt sorry for her so I sealed her in with a piece of Romaine lettuce & placed her on the window sill.

My scientific experiment plan was to see her produce less enemy babies through this torture.

A-hah! I was correct
she only made 5 enemy babies
I was jubilant & overjoyed!
mmmm...the more I torture them
the less production of their species
producing less sticky black spots
& invisible itchy bites
I couldn't wait to advertise the news!

I told my father about my experiment,
"Peuo, that is absolutely sinful
to treat our friends like that.
You watch in your next life time
you will be reincarnated into this insect!"

"But...Bok, we can't live with them. They get on my nerves! They are ruining my living space; our food. Disgusting!"

I was forced to listen to my father, forced to allow them to live with us symbiotically. We gave them permission to nurture & raise their families in our home for a few more years, paying no rent, eating our food for free, for 10 plus years.

They multiplied
in numbers
in the thousands
crawling
creeping
crawling in my bed sheets
shitting on my bed sheets
toilet
food
living room
tooth paste
clothes
toilet seats
toothbrush

This is totally GROSS!

Finally, after I graduated high school in 1997, my father realized that we couldn't live with them. After complaints from my mom, sisters & brothers we were going to finally get rid of these suckers!

He began plotting his counterintelligence platform. My father copied the scientific experiment plan – he got hold of my brother's Dixie cups

& lids, began cupping them himself! Every morning & night he would wake up at 3am & 9pm and he would spend an hour placing those nasty things in the cups!

My father was the ultimate leader – he organized a small army consisting of my nephews, nieces, my brother & myself.

We fought our enemies
cupped them
&
cupped them
in 10s, 20s, 30s...100s
we came full force
determined to win this war
the only stipulation my father had was,
"make absolute sure you don't slaughter them or else you will go to hell."
we would continue cupping
100's & 100's
we released them in the park
1/4 mile from our house

It was a victorious war, after 5 – 8 years of joining his counterintelligence army those nasty brown cockroaches were gone!

OUT OF MY LIFE!

Crab Apples

Driving on Interstate 495
in the quenching hot summer
we drive off onto the shoulder lane
lay our multi-colored pea cock straw mat
under cool shade
pull out our mortar & pestle
my older sister
meshing
chili peppers
salt
msg
sugar
makes a dipping
for our crab apples

We
my middle sister brothers aunt & I
climb crab apple trees
with our bare duck feet
holding on to branches like silly monkeys
we grab crab apples off branches
like big round green gum balls
we pop them in our mouths
tasting sour and bitter
ecstatic
looking below
we lightly throw them to Ma
gathering them off the ground
Ma takes them to Bok (Father)
he brings our fish sauce
fills it up
in our small Chinese red rose flowered bowl
dumps 6 spoonfuls of sugar
minces green red chili peppers
mixes msg

Bok pulls out our ivory-white cutting board
a butcher knife
lays them on the board
he smashes our crab apples
one
by
one
flattening them
allowing them to be dipped
in the fish sauce
moisturizing every white flesh
of our crab apple
with sweet & sour chili fish sauce

My older sister brings her chili salt dipping
closer to Bok
we climb off of the crab apple tree
picking up leftovers
off the ground
we happily sit
on our straw mat
dipping sweet & sour chili fish sauce
& chili-salt dipping
chewing & chowing & swallowing
on our crab apples
making smacking noises with our saliva, lips & tongue
each of us
remembering how it was to be back in our country
sitting on our multi-colored pea cock straw mat
under nice cool shade
eating our crab apples

We Stay Tight & Close at Sea

Digging clams
we
stand still
bend our knees
with our duck feet
on the ocean's floor
sand and gravel
tickling between our toes
feeling really good
with our sarongs
lifting up to our thighs
making indigenous
faces
jumping for joy

Digging snails
picking up
all sorts of sizes
black and stone-like
peeking through
we laugh
waiting for them
to peek again
grabbing with our
bare hands
we gather hundreds

Chasing crabs
tiny ones
medium ones
big ones
as the tide recedes
we wait for them to scurry back
on to the ocean's abode
we walk fast

picking them up
biting our dark-bronze
fingers
we make funny hurting faces

Fishing nets
we lay our nets on her
dark blue skin
watching for big fish
schools swim back and forth
waiting
we fold the fish net in half
gleeful
rejoicing
we are happy to
have some fish
in our nets

On Mother Earth's
gravel and sand
we make fires
bringing out pots
boiling water
placing our
crabs
snails
clams
in different pots
we make lime juice with salt and pepper
we
dip
&
dip
saliva
pouring out the corners
of our mouths
we munch

On Mother Earth's
gravel and sand
we scale our fish
slicing their stomachs open
taking out the unnecessary parts
sautéing them with Khmer spices
wrapping them in aluminum foil
poking holes
awaiting the steaming aroma
to cling to our noses
we eat happily
devouring
each cooked white flesh

Every summer
we go back to the ocean floors

Every summer
we always make our indigenous
happy faces

Every summer
we jump for emotional joy
to be with our family

Every summer
we can't wait
to share memories
to go back
laughing
smiling
munching
savoring
because family bonding is
our most important treasure

We stay tight and close
never letting go of
those good family times

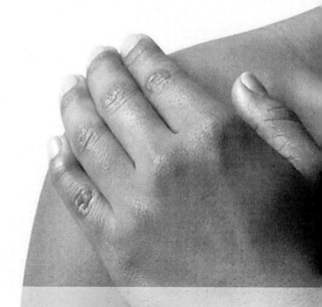

Bleaching My Skin

Bleaching My Skin

I hate her even in my sleep
dream I sharply slice her off
new fresh layers of white skin grow

I am forced to live with her
the sight of her makes me vomit

I consistently tell her she is too dark to be on me
but she insists it is not her fault
this color-haterism thing is biologically inherent

I buy
lightening cream
whiten her off of my face
praying it will dry her out
shedding off layers after layers after layers

In showers
I turn the dial to boiling hot
in order to burn her to death
from my face to my neckarmscheststomackbackbuttocksthighslegsfeet
I harshly scrub her off with a coarse cloth
dipped in sodium lauryl sulfate
burning her fiery red

I hate her!
I hate her!
I hate her!

Bitch! You deserve it!

Almost Ripe at 15

Tradition and Culture
say I am almost fit for marriage
we need to marry our daughter into a good family
we need to keep our pride and honor within our culture
wait a few more years they say
she cooks, cleans, and takes care of younger siblings
she is close to fitting our standards for arranged marriages

Almost Ripe
Yes, Almost Ripe

She just has to prove to us
that she will be a good wife
one that will always
cook, clean, and take care of her children
one that will always obey her husband
never talking back
never speaking her mind
allowing her husband
twice her age
to speak to her in a demeaning way
he makes all of the decisions

Yes, she is Almost ripe

Fitting the standards
of that wife
who is sub-sub-sub-missive
asking her husband for permission
to wear a certain outfit
to buy certain things
to go certain places...

Almost Ripe
Yes, Almost Ripe

I overhear this conversation my parents had
with a family friend
making promises to them
about marrying me to their son
whom I have not even met
they say Khmer daughters
need to return gratitude to their parents
this arranged marriage thing
is only to honor and appreciate the parents
marrying families
for economic reasons
marrying families
for honor is a family tradition
and it is to never be broken

Petrified and confused
I softly walk upstairs
wallowing in frustration
drowning out whispers of
Yes, she is Almost ripe for marriage.

No Sex in Our Constitution

Sex was a topic never discussed in our household
women with many boyfriends were sluts
disgusting whores with STDs written on their faces

in our constitution
boyfriends are not allowed
sex and children after marriage is a must
dating men will never be passed as an amendment
we are forced into unhappy arranged marriages
settling with the first person we meet

I grew up caged
barely looking at mirrors
hated my vagina
menstruation smelled bad
disliked my breasts
despised my dark nipples
my protruding buttocks
wanting to cut off fat from my thighs
excessively fanatic about losing weight

sexy
was out of the question
I felt like I was a sin

I was told
every part of my body needed to be covered & concealed
I covered myself with long sleeves & loose fitting jeans
I was defined like all the other Khmer women
I was definitely a sin to mother earth

Asian men said I was too dark to have sex with
they'd rather the Khmer-Chinese girls
or the Koreans
or the Chinese

my caramel complexion
dark nipples
dark vagina
flat nose
thick lips
outcasted me from Asian men

I turned to dating Black men
they accepted me
for who I was
wavy haired
brown skinned
full-lipped
flat nosed
dark nippled
woman

Dating Black men
hid my insecurities
having sex was crying a million times
I thought it promiscuous, sinful, ugly
I was still embarrassed by my vagina and dark nipples
I only wanted to have sex in the dark
he wouldn't have to see what my body really looked like

I was still a sin

Blackout

I had
sex with him
only in the dark

I was
embarrassed & ashamed
of my body

his black skin
didn't compliment
my caramel tone

all I could think about
was mommy & daddy
would not approve of this

Backlash

On a cold November day in 2001
I am scared
I brought a Black man home
to meet my parents

I want Daddy to accept Him
I want Mommy's approval
Daddy knows
He doesn't speak Khmer
or know
the culture
the food
the people
our traditions
our holidays
our mannerisms
"Daddy, he's just a nice guy who treats me well."

Daddy says *He's too dark, too Black*
I would make Black & Khmer babies
UGLY
says when she grows up & owns her own business
no one will support her
she will be too Black and not Khmer enough

Daddy slaps me
UGLY again
drops napalm on my love

Daddy wants his little girl
to marry within our culture

Daddy, "I'm all grown up.
We are living in America.
I am just dating him. I am not married to Him."

Daddy doesn't believe in dating
that's promiscuous
young Khmer women
are not allowed to open their legs like that

Mommy nods her head & agrees
she says nothing to me
her glances demand me to nod *yes*

I leave home crying profusely
feeling like Mommy & Daddy
were spies for the U.S. government

I tell Him that Mommy & Daddy don't like Black men
they're too dirty, too dark, and too poor

He wept angrily,
All my life I've been rejected because I am Black. I am used to it.

I Speak Only English

One morning
I wake up
I ask Daddy to teach me our language
Daddy goes outside to our farm
chops a thin flat rectangular wooden board
comes back into the house
writes the Khmer alphabet in white chalk

Daddy sits me down
after a 6 hour day of elementary school
takes his fingers and clasps them over mine
we point with our index fingers
at each Sanskrit character
reciting
singing almost

Next day
Daddy does the same
sits me down
takes his fingers
clasps them over mine
pointing each Sanskrit character
reciting
singing again almost

1 month later
Daddy does the same
this time backwards
this time concentrating on vowels
backwards and forwards a 100 times
sentences
word structures
pictures
memorizing

I roll my eyes
irritated at sitting on the floor
getting chalk dust all over my fingers

I walk away
"Daddy, I only read and write English!"

Daddy encourages me to continue
It's good to know two languages.

I try again
sitting
pointing
reciting
sitting
pointing
reciting

Annoyed, I get up
"Daddy Listen to me! I only write and read English!"

Daddy gave up
after countless hours
It's up to you. I am always here to teach you.

I walk away
refusing to learn the Khmer language
"Too many swiggly lines and circles, Daddy.
I can't remember them all."

I made a choice
to only learn how to read and write English

Now I barely know how to read or write Khmer
I wish I had listened to my Daddy.

The American-Only-Girl

I was that *little dark asian girl* who
no one could pronounce her name
> "how do you say your name?
> Pow
> Poe
> Pew
> Pooh?
> and your last name?
> Toy?
> Tie
> Too?"

I was that *little brown asian girl* who
bought Now & Later candies for the white kids
just so she could fit in

I was that *little dirty-colored asian girl* who
whined to her mother about brand name clothing
> like Gap
> Aeropostale
> American Eagle
> Nike
> Reebok

"Mom! You can't buy me these jeans, or these shoes, or this jacket!"
This is not pretty enough, not cool enough, and definitely not
expensive enough!"

I was that *chinky-eyed asian girl* who
got straight A's
the model minority

I was that *widened-her-eyes asian girl* who
spoke English with no accent
> "Were you born here?"
> "You speak English soooo well."

I was that *ridiculed cambodian girl* who
made noodles and fried rice for bake sale day
All the kids made fun of her

I was that *don't-wanna-be-khmer-girl* who
always felt outcasted
Her parents never went to any
       PTA meetings
       soccer games
       track meets
       open Houses

I was the *afraid-to-be-asian-girl*,
I wanted to be the *American-Only girl*
because the other kids' parents would always ask,
       "What do your parents do for a living?"
       "Oh, uh, my parents retired."
       "My dad was, uh, a technician."
       "My mom, uh..."
I would never finish this sentence

The truth was:
       I lied
       I lied because I felt I was not good enough
       I lied because I was disgusted by my parents

The truth was:
       I was the *poor, low class asian girl* whose
       family lived in the ghetto
       was on welfare
       and worked multiple jobs

The truth was:
       I was the *ashamed,* the *embarrassed asian girl*
       whose father and mother
       picked cans every day for a living
       every day in the hot, the cold, the rain, the snow

picked cans every day to send money to Cambodia to
build schools & temples
buy books & pencils
feed twenty-plus families

The truth was:
        I was the asian girl who hated herself for being un–American,
            who resented her parents
                    for not living the American Dream

Reminiscing Elementary

The white girls in my 5th grade class
always seemed to be better than me

I was invited to one of their birthday parties
I made my mother spend our welfare money
to buy her a nice gift
I wanted her to accept me

The white teachers
from kindergarten to 6th grade
always got nice gifts
on all of the American holidays
Again, I made my mother spend
our welfare and picking cans money
to buy my white teachers expensive gifts
so that I would always be the teacher's pet

Whenever my dad came to pick me up from school
I would make him wait at the corner
so that none of my white schoolmates would know
that my dad doesn't speak fluent English and is old and feeble

Before the school season would start
I would make my mother buy me
a pink Barbie doll lunch box
a pink thermos to match it
make American sandwiches
and buy oppressed cow's milk
I was ashamed to use my low-income meal tickets

When tests came around
I was told to study really hard to get straight A's
I did, but I still ain't rich

When gym day came around
I made sure I was the
fastest 50-yard-dasher
longest long jumper
strongest in pull bar
so that I would be liked
by all my white gym teachers

And then there were the white boys
I had a HUGE crush on one
his name was Martin
he was brunette, blue-eyed, and handsome
tall
dark
&
handsome
That was what I was told to fall in love with
I flirted with him and tried to convince him
that a dark-skinned asian girl like me
was better than those white skinny girls

I changed the pronunciation of my name
so all my white teachers and white classmates
wouldn't have a hard time saying it

Everyday when I woke up I made sure
I had the
latest kicks on
brand name jeans
dopest jackets
I wanted all the white kids to know
I ain't po'

I wanted to be like them
I would go home
bleach my skin
scrub it with hot water

rub excess darkness away
so that I would be lighter

just
like
them

Hate

She showed me how to love through:
    flat irons
    blow dryers
    sun-ins
    dyes
    gels
    sprays
    curling irons
    hot rollers
    perms
    wigs
    straighteners

She
didn't know
she was programmed
to kill her natural self

Loving Kamao

I Am Not Your Asian Exotic

I see...
Lotus drifting into steam-filled blue waters
Lotus drifting into refreshing lukewarm waters

I see pictures
I see images, childhood memories

floating, drifting...
drifting, floating...

I see my brown reflection
I see teary eyes

My mother always told me that I was too dark to be a Cambodian girl
that I will not be able to find a good husband
that I was too fat
that my nose was too flat
my lips were too big
my hair was too curly
my hips
my thighs
my fingers were
too this
too that
too this
too that

I was simply ugly

I was taught to hate myself
trained to love the ugly and hate the beautiful

Lotus just floating...
and drifting...

Slooooowly...
... into the whirlwind of dark blue waters

Two tongues
they say I was born with two tongues
taught by one
colonized by the other

For 24 years, I struggled to speak in Khmer to the elders
"Gyum."
"Uh . . . Gyum."
"Gyum, riep sor Boh, Meng."
"Greetings, Uncles and Aunts."

I retaliated with anger, tears, frustration
as my mother, father, brothers, and sisters told me that
I was too dark to be an Asian girl

"Ma . . . kamao saath!"
"Ma . . . kamao saath nah!"
I yelled and screamed at the top of my ferocious lungs,
"Mom . . . dark is beautiful!"
"Mom . . . dark is very beautiful!"
I am beautiful, Ma!
I am beautiful!

Two tongues
They say I was born with two tongues
I will use the colonized one to fight back!

No man will ever take my pride away from me!
I repeat
No man will ever take my pride!

I am not your Asian Exotic!
I am not your Asian submissive!
Not your Asian military honey!

Not your Asian sweetie!
I am not your Asian sex-me-up for $6 a night!

I will not starve myself!
I will not blonde my hair!
I will not widen my eyes!
Fix my nose!
My lips!
My breasts!
My thighs!
My hips!
My color!
My accent!

I WILL NOT KILL the Asian body the way that you want me to!

Two tongues
They say I was born with two tongues
I will use them both to fight back!

Kum min thwer thay!
Kum min thwer thay!

I refuse!
I refuse!
I REFUSE TO KILL   ME!

I am a strong Cambodian womyn
with plenty of Cambodian pride
I will forever heal my soul
My heart
My mind
My body with love!

I am beautiful, Ma!

Ma, *I am beautiful!*

Playing in the Sun

Growing up I took hot showers
with my panties, bra, sarong on
I never looked at my body

Now I take showers   naked
cherishing the indigenous body
my Goddess of Life gave me

When I got my period at 13, I was told
let all the red poison release
never bathe until it was gone
even if you smell foul

Now I embrace my womb
releasing a part of me monthly
this is my Womynhood

My nipples   dark
I used to scrub them
in order to whiten them

Now I feel proud
my Khmer-African blood gave me
these gifts to feed my unborn children

My face   brown
I was given lightening cream
I smeared it all over for 18 years

Now I wear my brown skin
thrilled to play in the sun!

My hair
I used to bleach it
wring its natural-ness away

Now I wear my curls down
happy

I now wear me in our village
standing tall
I smile
proud to be who I am

I now play in the sun
no long sleeves
no hat to cover my face
wearing me in my village
standing tall
I smile wide

I now play in the sun
letting those know
that it is the most
peaceful and self-fulfilling feeling to love yourself

Fat Girl to Skinny Girl...

At 5 feet, 2 & ½ inches
I went from stick skinny
to that just right genie bottle
to that "oh you're soooo cute" chubby girl
to "damm, your thighs are brushing against each other"

FAT GIRL

I was fighting with my own silent eating disorder
undiagnosed at 19; weighing almost 150 lbs

FAT FAT FAT

I shot up piles of sugar, fats, oils in my veins
escalated from a size 4 to a 6, 8,10 to an almost 12

GIANT GIANT GIANT

I was depressed. Severely depressed.

I placed on layers of make-up
shrugged off the weight quickly
zoomed from a 12 to a 10, 8, 5/6, skipped a 3/4
vacuuming my fat to a 1/2
with no hips, butt, thighs
in a matter of 30 days I lost them all
I carried heavy loads of dark saggy bags under my eyes

SKINNY GIRL

I thought of SUICIDE.

.

...To That Just Right Girl

5 years ago I was battling obesity and anorexia. FAT, GIANT, Skinny, and Suicide – thoughts were just bad nightmares. I thought I had to be that chopstick-looking-girl in order to attract friends and men; that I had to have a certain body type in order to be gawked and stared at in a sexual way. I was climbing an indefinite set of stairs and it kept me panting. I was constantly out of breath because all I could think about then was that I needed to satisfy society and fit standards. I became so tired of trying to please others and do and become what others want so I decided to find my own path.

I am That Just Right Girl because my healing journey begins by writing poems, exercising my mind/body, drinking lots of water, digesting protein, fruits, and vegetables, and singing to myself. I am in a better place because I laugh and smile indefinitely, reconnect with family, read books, participate in women's healing groups, talk to those I trust, and hang out with friends.

I am that Just Right Girl because I get manicures, pedicures, wear sexy maroon-colored heels, hot pink mini skirts, see -through flowy shirts, and wear my hair frizzy/crazy wild. I am much happier because I no longer place layers of make-up over my depression, no longer zoom from a 12 to a size 0.

I am that Just Right Girl because I am confident, loving, caring, charming, intelligent, and wise.

To me I am perfect.

She is the Yellow Rose

Dedicated to Salin Nuth

She swarmed me with yellow roses
my best friend since 5 years old

I smacked Her back with envy & jealousy
angry at white pure skin & Chinese eyes
long lustrous shiny straight hair

She kept flowering me with radiant rays of sunshine
She fought back when others
threw gasoline on my dark skin
I threw thumb tacks on Her face
hoping to make holes
make Her ugly
I was furious at Her beauty, it enchanted men

I hated Her
I hated Her kind-heartedness
it charmed our elders
echoed Khmer tradition

She never knew how I felt all these years
we were best friends

At 18 years old, I chose to shred our friendship
leaked its blood in the cracks of canyons

I ran away from home
insecure, I envied other women
who I felt would steal
my happiness
my men
my beauty
my Khmer traditional ways

I was angry, very angry
In my dreams, I longed for Her yellow roses

She was a genuine best friend
I threw her away

I made a mistake
I am very sorry

It has been 8 years since I left Her hanging

I picked up the phone and called Her
confessed to my insecurities
stirred them up
volcanic reactions burst into mounds of truth
formed a lake of tears on my lap

I told Her why I avoided Her for so long
asked Her for forgiveness
She grieved with me
accepted my flaws
told me she still loved me unconditionally

We talked about the silly things we used to do
1980s punk rock hair styles
baggy, multi-colored jeans
tight mini skirts
red lipstick
stole my sister's heels
played Tiffany & Debbie Gibson a million times
made up our own music videos

We laughed and giggled
sat & talked on the phone for hours
made poetry
in our own way

taught each other
childhood truths through
our voices
our words
our honesty

To Pledge or Not to Pledge

I pledge allegiance to the flag of the United States of America...

And sing the lyrics to the Star Spangled Banner,
Oh say can you see...by the dawn's early light...

Cambodian, Vietnamese, and Laotian families were evacuated from our home countries and I find myself in 1983 honoring the American flag through pre-school, elementary, junior high, and high school.

I celebrate all the HOLY – Days
Christmas
Thanksgiving
Easter
Valentine's Day
Mother's Day
Father's Day

Christmas
I find my family spending thousands of dollars buying love. If I didn't get the most expensive gift I would throw a fit. I will never forget the only man who was my savior. He would bring gifts, love, and happiness on his reindeers.

We cannot buy love, compassion, and kindness.
There is no man on reindeers in a red suit with a white beard.

Teach your children the truth.

Thanksgiving
My teachers taught me that them Anglo people helped the Native American Indians. They told me that these people died because they did not know how to cure themselves from smallpox. They did not tell me was that smallpox was brought here from the white people's country.

Teach your children the truth.

Easter
I never understood the concept of blue, yellow, pink, red eggs.
I just left that in the 5th grade.

Valentine's Day
On this day couples get together to dine at four-star restaurants,
buy dozens of flowers, rent fancy hotels, vacation at touristy spots.
Bling, Bling, "Here comes the bride..."

Whatever happened to homemade dinners, listening with compassion,
nurturing, caring, honesty, respect? We need to make love every day.
Without it we are dying.

Teach your children.

Mother's and Father's Day
I never understood why we only celebrated mothers and fathers.
Why is it only once a year? Whatever happened to Sisters, Brothers,
Aunts, Uncles, Friends, Ancestors?
Did we forget to put them on the calendar?

Teach your children.

I was taught about how great Christopher Columbus was.
He discovered Amerikkka! I was taught the Mormons claimed Utah
as their promised land. I was not taught the American Indians were
warriors fighting to keep their land.

I was taught that African people were slaves – not humans.
That being Black was a curse. That being a Black womyn gave the slave
master every right to rape and molest. I was not taught about how
powerful Rosa Parks was, how skillful Nat Turner was, how organized
the Black Panthers were.

I was taught that Puerto Rico was a commonwealth, and the U.S.
could dictate their lives. I was not taught about Vieques – a bombing
site for future wars; about the sterilization of Boricua womyn.

Asian and Asian American History. Forget this Shit!!!
It was never considered a subject.

The only thing I was taught was that Chinamen built the railroads.

They didn't teach me about
how the majority of Ho Chi Minh's souljahs
were womyn fighting in flip-flops in the Vietnam War
about Yuri Kochiyama and her strength to protest
the Japanese internment camps;
about my mother & father who saved eight lives
during the genocide in Cambodia
about Vincent Chin who was beaten to death!

I was taught that wars were needed to protect this country;
that violence on violence is the answer.

I was never taught about broken families, people dying, starving.

We should think twice before we honor the flag
and sing the Star Spangled Banner.

And before you put your children to bed,
Teach them your truth.

She Raises Her Shovels and Hoes High

Dedicated to the Vietnamese Women and People

At 15, she ties her charcoal stringy hair with a thick blade of rice grass.
Null 'n void of embroidered flowers her straw hat is raw & rugged.
Cotton negrito capri pants/fitted shirts she slips boned-feet
into her flip-flops carrying a knapsack.

Mid -1960's,
Uncle Ho orders his villages to protect North Vietnam
the U.S. is invading
70,000 plus
Mothers
Wives
Daughters
Sisters enlist

She raises her shovels and hoes high
marching flip-flop style through exotic roads
she treks through wild animals, poisonous snakes,
deadly plants, and foreign invaders

She is the 12.7 mm, anti-aircraft guns
pointing from factory hill tops
she shoots American planes with sharpened tongues

She is your Machine Gunner. On mountainous cliffs,
she spits out staccato sounds ejecting bullets:
"Go Back to Your Own Country Muthafucker!"

Flip-flop fighting!
Artillery Warriors!
In deep ravines, black ornaments painted onto disheveled hair
avoiding air raids; she uses hidden cannons and missile launchers.

She is your Quilted Cadre, gallivanting through jungle woods,
lugging 30 kilograms of bricks up mountain slopes.

Using her shovels and hoes, she rebuilds Uncle Ho's destructive trail.
She uses her body as a plank to keep trucks and ammunition moving.

She is your Lieutenant
the AK-47, 7.62mm
She shoots thousands

"This is my land. I will not lose!"

She is the Vietnamese Woman
fighting wars in flip-flops

She lives with leeches
eats leaves and grass
uses safety pins to catch catfish

She witnesses comrades die of starvation
sees floating dead bodies in streams
bombs blow her up

She dies for honor...

Liberating Vietnam
We sing sultry songs over bonfires

Chanting
Our voices louder than bombs
Our voices louder than bombs

Buddha gives blessings
to the live and dead ones

Chanting
Our voices louder than bombs
Our voices louder than bombs

April 1975 – the invaders leave after 10 years
our country ruined
3.5 million dead

Mothers spread bodies like molded strawberry paste
Fathers Headless
broken hearts and kisses
are thrown in deep abysses
They are gone...
They are gone...

300,000 children orphaned

She is now 25
hallucinations & nightmares
Agent Orange deforms babies
legs twist, eye lids patched
lips fall below the chin

4 million disabled

Platoon Leader seeks companionship/family
She never ever weds
never experiences love
She lives in stalking loneliness
He says, "NO!", to her virgin body
Her venomous body unfit for marriage
She produces retarded babies

700,000 plus wounded souljahs

Scarred by chemical warfare
death is always a promise
Malaria turns her into faded yellow/thinning hair
She is dying

We
relive Vietnam
as if it was
As if it is
to-day
yester-day
yester-year
or 30 years ago

We
pay honor and tribute to our sisters
We never forget our She-roes

Remember...
70,000 plus
Mothers
Wives
Daughters
Sisters
raising shovels and hoes high
marching flip-flop style through exotic roads

Spitting Out White Cum

We have been stepped on by your cotton-white ass!

From beauty standards
to sun-kissed blonde hair
to pointy straight-lined nose
to an almost chopstick figure
to *Maybe It's Maybeline*
to *Easy, Breezy, Beautiful ... Cover Girl*

My people's minds are chained in wires that leave Yellow blood
dripping...
        One by One
        One by One

Do you understand how much you've destroyed?
        Exoticism
        Orientalism

You tell me and the Asian womyn in this world
how different we are
how sexually exotic we look,
so you could inject your sausage into our bodies
and leave us hanging

You tell me and the Asian womyn in this world
how much you love us
how much you adore us
so you could squirt your dirty venom into our mouths
and leave us tearing

We, Orientals, as you profoundly stated in your English dictionary,
        of OR characteristic of the Orient (sometimes offensive)

It's always offensive mutherfucker!
Just like when you call me chink,

It's always offensive!
Just like when you call me an exotic oriental slut,
It's always offensive!
Just like when you call my Asian brothas asexual,
It's always offensive!

Asian womyn:
we are figures of material wealth

| We | are | a | commodity |
| We | are | | commodities |

Asian womyn:
We are a thing
        to be tossed out when we are not needed
        to be walked on by dirty feet
        to be displayed in cabinets and museums

Asian womyn:
We are

        rugs
        antiques
        sculptures
        pictures

Asian womyn:
We are

        used
        abused
        slapped Around
        shipped Around

You embellish and are proud
        of destroying
        of taking
        of killing

Muthafucker!

You need to understand that I will NOT let you:
  Colonize me
  rape me of all my culture
  appropriate my ethnic pride
  kill my mind
  denigrate my feelings
  tell me that I'm ugly
  dictate my life

"Do you understand the words that are coming out of my mouth?"

Yellow Whores

Smack That Yellow Pussy Real Hard!

White and Dominant
he fucks her
she is 9, thin and fragile

Asian and Dominant
he fucks her
sucking the tiny hairs off her breast
she is not even 12

1932
he hops on the comfort wagon to Shanghai
grabs China Doll
ties her wrists
pries her stick-skinny brown legs
injects molded milky venom
into her precious womb

1957
Thailand –
at 7 years her mother sells her to the brothel in the city
she is number 20,001
$80/month sent to the countryside
to feed her family
she is a slut for 20 more years

1967
Vietnam –
he conquers land
bringing erectile dickful of
G.I. soldiers to rape
slanted-eyed dociles
she induces heroin in order
to fuck 10 per night

Filipinas – continue the legacy
he sucks pussy juice
squirting speed into his mouth
he spits her $6

Laos – she intoxicates herself
        Remy
        Vodka
        Hennessy
she is no longer shy
he demands to stick her
even when she's bleeding
she has no choice
she will be fined by the brothel master

Japan –
he slaps her face 4 times
she asks him to put on a condom
he weighs 250
she 110
she takes barbiturates
lays there
he now owns her

Cambodia –
she calls him in
one after another
making sure he's an American
she hopes to fulfill
her American dreams

2003 – New York City
I remember
New Year's Eve
I was intoxicated
he brought me to his room
slowly slipped his hands into my jeans

"NO!"
"Yes!"
"NO! GET THE FUCK OFF ME!"

I tried to fight him
my clothes were on the floor

I pushed him off
he pushed forward

Forward
Forward

I struggled
but he was much stronger
I stopped and laid there

Sobbing...

Sobbing...

Sobbing...

Abort

Laying on that chair my legs wide open
tears drip from the corner of my almond eyes

He injects foreign instrument
sucks my seed from my womb

I lay there, silently yanking my hair
trying to erase the sonogram images

I cry in bed
I killed her

There are no more symptoms of motherhood

Feeling empty and sinful
my tears are thunder

Smiles are frowns
my womb is empty

she is gone

I am sorry
I am so sorry

I did
what was best for me

Black Curls

jet black in color
her essence is juniper

void of poisonous chemicals
she grows

layer after layer
she falls in complete love with herself

it took 16 years to break free
from excessive dyes, chemicals, and hair tools

she is now pure
worn without hesitation

she will never again be that lunatic
who once destroyed her inheritance

Salvation

Ancestors' Whispers

The blood of my Khmer ancestors

descends on white feather paper

whispering,

Daughter, tell our story for us.

I sketch my name with their blood

P

E

u

0

Pen

in the palm of my hands

I write words

tell stories

of

my life

their past...

I Am Sorry

In his saffron bright orange robe,
he sits in lotus pose
wrinkled cinnamon brown hands, palms facing each other
slightly touching light burgundy brown lips
he speaks a chant
praying to Buddha

Ma sits in semi-lotus pose a few steps away from the monk,
being careful not to touch him,
her wrinkled tannish-brown hands
palms facing each other touching her tiny reddish – pink lips
she speaks a chant
praying to Buddha

I sit in an unsettling semi-lotus beside Ma,
feeling uncomfortable I stare at the statue of Buddha
& my used-to-be father
he is no longer my father
I don't know why he has given himself to the monastery
I mumble gibberish chants
half praying to Buddha

I cry silently
wondering why my father has not come home
he hates us
we are not good children
my mother is not a good mother

For the next 2 years,
I sit again & again with Ma
feeling uncomfortable
missing my father
she misses her husband

I think he's an unworthy father

One day, Ma & I pick him up from the monastery
he dresses himself up in a silk-worm sampot
sewn with purple & red lines
a beige button down shirt
packs his bags
slips his feet into
dark blue flip-flops
and joins us in the car

Ma has a huge smile on her sweet round face

During our car ride home he says he has transformed
he has committed to staying away from
smoking
drinking
gambling
verbally abusing his children
& will continue
to give offerings and honor our ancestors
to pray to Buddha

I cry honestly,
"I am sorry for making all these assumptions about you leaving us."

I am now at peace knowing my father speaks
truths of
love
honesty
respect
for his family and friends
our community
our ancestors
by way of Buddhism

I will never make those cruel assumptions about him again.

Dear Mother

From sunrise to sunset
you breast fed me in the rice field

Under our bamboo-stilted home,
laying nested in your arms in our handmade hammock
you lulled me to sleep singing songs of beauty

You sat under our tamarind tree in your lotus sarong
on your hands and knees
making porridge soup

Dear Mother

I remember You
braiding my jet-black hair
twisting and turning

I remember You
rolling egg rolls
stir-frying hoison marinated rice noodles
smiling

I remember You
sitting Indian-style on our mahogany-wooden floors,
chalking Sanskrit letters

And I remember You
proud to be a Khmer Mother
a Khmer womyn

You're
Strong
Wise
Beautiful

Keeping our culture alive

Dear Mother

I am swimming miles with you
crossing glistening oceans
returning to our ancestral land

I am traveling with you into poppy fields
holding hands
laughing

Mother,
you are perfectly beautiful with your
duck feet
coarse grey hair
brown skin

You are my souljah
always fighting for love
speaking truths to life

Mother,
you have taught me to love myself through
harsh realities
heart breaks
suffering
change

Mother,
I thank you for you

Running Water & Soap Suds

My Grandmother's mocha colored hands mingle with soap suds underneath running water like subtle waterfalls making white bubbles. She puts my Mother's green peacock sarong in the wooden bucket. Her two hands grab each end — rubbing, wringing out dirt, lathering. More bubbles. She does this repeatedly, taking each section, rubbing, wringing until it is dirt-free. She hangs it on our hemp rope leaving the sun to pour out heat & the wind to sway it dry.

She passes her mocha colored hands to my Mother. She, too, mingles them with soap suds & running water washing my green peacock sarong. She sweats under the quenching sun, never complaining, rubbing, wringing out the natural stains of daily life, draining dirt, until it is dirt-free, hanging it to be dried by the wind & the sun.

I watch for years learning this tradition. My Mother told me she retained this tradition from Her Mother whom I have never met.

I watch her for years so that I can pass my mocha colored hands mingled with soap suds & running water, wash a green peacock sarong for my unconceived daughter... rubbing, wringing soiled fabric, recollecting generations of women in my family practicing the same ritual.

This is how we honor our culture.

Khyum
Salangh Bok

Kisses in the Coffin

I never once told him I love him

khyum salangh Bok, I whispered

I puckered my lips,
kissed his cold cheeks
in his glossy-mahogany-wooden coffin

I fixed his white collar
and lightly patted his frizzy white cotton hair
holding his hands tightly

when he was alive
I never once gave him a kiss
ever in my life

at least this time I did before we burned him

Daddy's Laundry List for Life

1.   two pairs of sompot (men's long skirt)
2.   a few pairs of his light weight cotton white shawls
(the ones that older Khmer men wear as shirts on hot summer nights)

3.   2 pairs of grey slacks
4.   3 white button down long sleeve shirts

5.   a few pairs of grey sweat pants and sweat shirts
(that we got him for Christmas because that's all he would want)
6.   one blue Thailand brand, "last a lifetime" kind of flip-flops

7.   one pair of dark grey velcro sneakers from Ames
(our local department store)
8.   one pair of dirty excessively used sneakers
(for his picking cans days)

9.   a Khmer – English dictionary
10.   his 50 cents, 8 ½ x 11" blue lined store brand notebook

11.   a few black and blue pens
12.   reading glasses

13.   stainless steel rusty tweezer
14.   one Panasonic dual recording cassette player
15.   dozens of recorded/memorized Theravada Buddhism
        chants and prayers
16.   glossy beautiful paper portraits of Buddha sitting
        on a lotus flower

17.   his twin size bed and his one of a kind flat pillow

18.   his 10 children and 30 plus grandchildren,
        in the U.S. and abroad

19.   his wife

My First Best Friend

We became best friends
the ones who liked and disliked one another
through 28 years of arguments, disagreements
through that silent passive-aggressiveness

I revolted
His words
His Daddy ways

I wanted to be me
He wanted me to be someone else
that cultural-submissive-daughter

He preached,
good daughter
only does what good daddy says

He scolded me
for not cooking and cleaning enough

We kept arguing

He kept giving me that
disgraceful look
he disowned me
because I did not turn out to be that good Daddy's girl

Daddy, I just want to be me
I want to go to the movies with my friends
put on pretty make-up
especially, that blood-shot red lipstick like the Japanese Geisha dolls
dress up in that lacey-sexy tight blue shirt/black cotton- mini skirt
play soccer because it makes me feel confident
voice my opinion

Daddy, I just want you to understand
I want to date boys (and give that special one kisses)
not tied down to one immediately

Daddy, please...
I want to dye my hair like all the other girls
blonde highlights, hues of cinnamon, hints of almond-espresso colors
wear heels because it makes me feel tall and ultra sexy
put on that tight curvaceous red dress
and just feel like that pretty little girl with a pretty little figure

Daddy, Listen! Please!
I know I never told you
but
I want you to tell me that you love me
I want you to allow me to tell you that I love you

Daddy, I'm begging you!
I want you to hug me and tell me -
I'm the best baby girl you will ever have

Please, Daddy...
accept me for who I am
because you are my best friend

Blue Light

He couldn't burn wood like he used to back in Cambodia
so he turned on our Maytag stove

click click click

blue-reddish-yellow tones
made our home
warm
hot and crisp
for the winter months

5 Cents

For over two decades, Mom & Dad saved every penny from welfare,
food stamps, under the table jobs, and from picking cans

A routine in Lowell, Chelmsford, and other
nearby Massachusetts towns
3X a day
4AM   9AM   8PM

North, South, East, West

2 liters, 1 liter, coke, pepsi, sprite, gingerale cans & plastic bottles...
budweiser, heineken, bud light, coors & coors light bottles...

Noon to 1PM – Redemption Centers
Packing, sorting, bagging, separating

5 cents   5 cents   5 cents   5 cents
small   medium   large   extra large bottles
they collected them all
never embarrassed, always proud

5 cents put food on the table for our family
5 cents helped build temples
5 cents donated to poor schools
5 cents supported the daily living of the people in our village
back in Cambodia

5 cents has been embedded in my mind
as a symbol of respect, honor, love, care, and hard-work
a couple who dedicated their energy to help those in need

5 cents 5 cents 5 cents 5 cents

Condensed Milk w/ Italian & French Bread

At Market Basket
off of exit 38, Interstate 495
He buys his weekly 99 cent
white Italian and French bread
with his 2 for $1 sweet succulent can of condensed milk

He in his blue flip-flops
dark grey ten-year-old slacks
halfway buttoned white collar long sleeve cotton shirt
wears his naturally drawn happy face
walks by aisle 9
picks up two 99 cent 3 liter Market Basket brand coke & orange soda
gallivanting 2 aisles to his right
sweeps up 2 cans of super sweet condensed milk
still wearing his shining smile

5 minutes later he quickly skips
to the bakery section and grabs his
nice warm Italian & French bread from the woven wooden basket
made fresh early in the morning
still kept warm in a 2 feet
recycle white umbrella-like vertical white paper bag
He then proceeds to pay for them at the cashier's check-out

He walks to our beat up silver Jeep Laredo
holding a brown plastic Market Basket bag filled with his favs
always walking, slightly dragging his blue flip-flops, head straight up
wearing his shining smile

Pomegranates

During every fall and winter, He used to get so ecstatic when they were in season. He would purchase them at the nearby Khmer food market and drive them back with him in our beat-up/rusty sliver 1984 Jeep Laredo. Hurriedly, He would rush to the kitchen and prepare them.

He used to slice them down the middle in half with our chipped, overly used butcher knife, atop our used blood and vegetable stained plastic cutting board. Blood/fuchsia blended colors, juices oozing out he gets really ecstatic (yes, really!), smiling, oh soooo elegantly with glands salivating, natural spit, dripping out from the corners of his maroon-purple lips. He would place them in our plastic red painted floral Chinese bowl.

Yum!

Turning on our black Sony 20 inch television, wearing his long dark/ blue silver grey stripe sompot, white button down collar dress shirt, untucked, and blue flip-flops, He sits on the couch, turning on the weather channel, staring & watching

while he -

Munches
Cracks
Smacks

Yum! Yum! Yummy!

As He munches cracks smacks the pomegranate seeds in his mouth His unstoppable smile lights the entire room

we are happy
the fresh pomegranate seeds
make my father so happy

His Feet

His wrinkled, bruised, callused, aching, over-abused
dark brown feet
narrate 75 years of his life

He was sitting on the F train on that orange seat
wearing a pair of blue flip-flops
my father always used to wear in our home growing up

I didn't know him but I was
stealing glimpses of his presence
hoping he will not notice

He made me meditate on my deceased father
I wept silently
hoping no one saw me
hiding & dodging his looks

Ash & creases in his feet
I wanted to memorize the lines & the dirt in every corner
so I quickly read the ash and creases thoroughly
hoping that he didn't hop off the next stop

Please Sir,
stay on the F train for 30 more minutes

I need you
I really do

help me bring him back with a beating heart
just for a little more

Please Sir,
Please

Bok, Rest Peacefully

Morphine drip drip drip drip...

Oxycontin 30 mg
Colace
Zophran
Megase
Lactolose
Oxygen tank
Clotrimazole
Blood transfusions
Asthma pumps
Hydrocortisone
Tylenol

Salt water drip, drip, drip, drip...

HE

on his bed

stuck

Fragile bones
A non-functioning left arm
Stick-skinny legs
Flabby arms
Cloudy eyes
Constipation
Lungs filled with water
Liver no longer works
Blood does not flow

His heart stopped beating...

The only thing left he loved on his body
were his tiny white cotton-colored hairs

I will never forget the day I cried profusely
lung cancer has been eating my father for months

We did not know
it was too late to save him

Bok, Rest Peacefully

We will never forget the day you
risked your life
to take 8 people out of the Killing Fields
to find us grains of rice when we were starving in the refugee camps
to learn simple English to pass the test
and put us on that 24 hour plane ride to America

We will never forget the days
you worked & worked & worked & worked
to put food on the table

We will never forget the days
you embraced Buddhism
to rid yourself of the negativity & toxins
to bring peace, harmony, and love to your children and wife

We will never forget the days
you taught us to always give
and not do wrong to others

Bok, Rest Peacefully

I will never forget the days
you drove in our beat up 6 passenger Buick
to pick me up from elementary school

I will never forget
how & when you taught me the Khmer & English alphabet
on wooden cardboard, written in white chalk

I will never forget
our subtle & loving disagreements
about how life should be

I will never forget
the day you brought me be back to Cambodia in 2000
to see what it really means to be Khmer
to speak & breathe our culture

Bok,
We will never forget you

Bok,
I will never forget you

you will never be forgotten

Bok, Rest Peacefully

Acknowledgements

Thank you Timothy Prolific Jones, Manuvaskar Kublall, Eternal Love, Howard Treadwell, Karl Kellman, Phearuth Tuy, Camilo Gaston-Greenberg, Khayree Jannah, Robin Taylor Bryant, Monal Pathak, and Kahlil Almustafa for your continued love and support throughout the different stages of *Khmer Girl*. *Khmer Girl* made it because of all your dedicated hard work and in believing in my story.

Thank you.

Glossary

Khmer – [pronounced kuh-mai] the primary ethnic group in Cambodia. For the purposes of this book, the word Khmer also represents people of Khmer origin and descent.

Cambodia – formerly known as Kampuchea, is a country in Southeast Asia that borders Thailand to the west and northwest, Laos to the north, Vietnam to the east, and the Gulf of Thailand to the south.

Battambang –is a province in Cambodia. In this province lies one of the districts (srok) Thmor Koul, one of the communes Kouk Khmum, and one of the villages (phum) Chhkae Koun; Chhkae Koun is where the Tuy family grew up.

Killing Fields – multiple sites where the Khmer Rouge killed or brought hundreds of thousands of dead Khmer bodies to be buried.

Pol Pot – also known as Saloth Sar; died on April 15, 1998; leader of the Khmer Rouge regime communist party, inducted a revolutionary program to "clean" Cambodia through agrarian collectivization; was Prime Minister of Democratic Kampuchea from 1976–1979; his rule resulted in the deaths of an estimated 1.7 to 2.5 million people.

Khmer Rouge – Pol Pot's communist party that ruled Cambodia, 1975-1979.

Peuo – [pronounced pbaou] the youngest child in a Cambodian family. Although, Phearea was my birth given name, I was called Peuo for the majority of my life and kept the name. There are many variations of the spelling of "Peuo" when translated to English.

Phearea – [pronounced pearrea] my birth given name, a sour fruit in Cambodia but when ripe it is sweet.

Tuy – [pronounced thuy] the Tuy's family last name, and my paternal grandfather's first name. It is normally a tradition in Khmer culture to give the grandfather's first name as the grandchildren's last name.

Bok – Father

Khyum – respectful way to say "I"

Salangh – love

Kamao – dark or black in color

Sampot – men's Khmer long skirt, normally worn in the house.

Bong Barouh – older brother

Paoun Srei – younger sister

Sarong – a long usually colorful and floral skirt worn in the house by Khmer women and young girls.

Khyum min thwer thay – "I refuse"

About the Author

Peuo [bpaou] **Tuy** is a Khmer-American woman born in Cambodia in 1979. At the age of 12, she began journaling about being a young Khmer girl growing up in Lowell, Massachusetts. A writer of narrative poetry, she recounts memories of being a young immigrant and refugee girl from her childhood, adolescent and early adult life, constructing a poignant story of pain, passion, love, courage and triumph.

She has traveled across the country utilizing poetry as a vehicle to expose and educate audiences to the realities of growing up as a dark-skinned Asian woman in America. Venues that have featured Peuo as a performer include The University of California Los Angeles, The Nuyorican Poets Café, Nuves, The Sugar Shack, the Harlem Book Fair, Freeport High School; Philadelphia's North by Northwest and Slam Garden; Hunter College, the University of Massachusetts Amherst, Northwest Carolina University, and Rutgers University New Brunswick, amongst others. Peuo was a member of Urbintel's *HerStory* cast, which toured universities and performance venues on the East Coast, from Boston to North Carolina.

She holds a Bachelor of Arts in Africana, Puerto Rican and Latino Studies from Hunter College (CUNY), and a minor in Asian-American Studies.